Adventures of Larry Lamppost and friends

Mark L'estrange

Adventures of Larry Lamppost & Friends
Published in 2022 by Mark L'estrange

Copyright © Mark L'estrange

ISBN 978-1-7399249-3-5

Illustrations by Pachyderm Tales,
Illustrated by Parvathi N Venkitaraman
Book design & publishing services provided by JM Agency
www.jm.agency

Adventures of Larry Lamppost and friends

A little note from Mark

Welcome to a collection of children's stories I started to write a few months ago. I created them for my own children and I decided to compile them into this short book. Each story can be read or told on its own in about 10 minutes and I really hope you and your child have as much fun with them as me and my children.

Contents

Larry Lamppost & Family

This is a story about Larry Lamppost and his brothers, and how their family name had a funny link to their accidents! There were four brothers in the family, Larry was the eldest, Peter aged eight, Luke six and Adam aged seven.

Larry was in school one day and was mad busy doing his favourite subject, maths. Not really. He absolutely hated maths! But it was soon time to leave and he was looking forward to that.

He would skateboard to school all the time and he skateboarded home too. After school he couldn't wait to hurry home to play with his friends. So when the bell went, he grabbed his skateboard and as fast as he could, he set off home. But when he was nearly there, he was not looking where he was going and you'll never guess what happened … That's right, he went crash, bang, right into a lamppost! Ouch!

His brother, Peter just happened to be passing by and saw Larry hit the lamppost and he fell around laughing at him. When they got home, Peter told the other brothers, Adam and Luke what happened to poor Larry, and they all made fun of him. Poor Larry.

The following day at school, Larry happened to have a much better time. He passed all his exams and so was in great form. He was much more relaxed today as he skateboarded for home and while rolling down the pavement, he saw his younger brother, Luke and waved over to him. Luke was on his bike at the time and when he turned to wave back to Larry, his front wheel banged into, you'll never guess what... that's right... a lamppost! Luke fell off his bike and landed on the path.

Larry ran over to Luke but did not laugh or make fun of him like his brothers had done to him yesterday; Larry was worried and wanted to know if his brother was ok. Luke got up rubbing his arm, but apart from that he was OK. He was more concerned about what the others would think of him, so pleaded with Larry not to tell the rest what happened.

"I won't tell," said Larry, "on one condition. You stop making fun of me when things like this happen... like they seem to a lot with lampposts!" Luke agreed, so Larry and Luke became best of friends after that, and often had a good old laugh about their mishaps with lampposts.

Another day, two of the brothers, Peter and Adam were out playing on the road near their house when a bully,

Nigel, came up and started picking on Adam. Nigel had his gang behind him. They were all bullies who would only pick on kids smaller than them.

Larry, being the eldest of the Lamppost brothers always looked out for his younger siblings and on this day he was out skateboarding with his best friend Johnny No Shoes when they saw Adam and Peter being picked on by Nigel. Larry and Johnny were older than the bullies, and when the bullies saw them coming over they all ran. Larry went to see if his brothers were ok, but Adam was crying.

"What happened Adam?" asked Larry and Johnny.

When Adam eventually stopped crying, he told them. "Nigel robbed my favourite football."

Larry was annoyed. "That's it," he said, "we are tired of Nigel and the rest of his bully friends picking on smaller children, but they always run away. We need to teach them a Lamppost lesson!" It would be a real lamppost lesson for Nigel, but you'll have to wait as to why!

They could see Nigel and his gang on the next block, still bullying other children.

"You go up to Nigel and say you want your ball back." said Larry to Adam, explaining the plan. "We will stay here next to the wall, hidden behind this lamppost."

Adam was nervous approaching the big bully but knew that the others weren't far away. When he got to Nigel, he said bravely, "Give me back my ball."

Nigel said in his bully voice ,"MAKE ME."

Larry Lamppost and Johnny No Shoes ran up to Nigel and his bully friends and Nigel's face dropped immediately. He had nowhere to run this time.

Larry said, "I believe you have something that belongs to my brother."

Nigel replied in a shivery and quiet voice, "Sorry, here it is Larry." and rolled the ball to him.

The children who Nigel had just been bullying were now happy and so was Adam to have his favourite ball back. Larry and Johnny made Nigel and his wimpy friends say sorry to everyone they'd been bullying. They also got the ringleader and the gang to promise Peter, Adam and Luke and all the local kids that they would never bother them again.

Nigel couldn't get away fast enough on his bike, and was looking behind himself and can you guess what happened to him? He slammed straight into a lamppost! Larry turned to Luke laughing, saying, "Looks like we are not the only family that have problems with lampposts!"

The End

Mr. Shopper's Christmas

There once lived a family called the Shoppers. Mr and Mrs Shopper had two sons called John and Peter and a daughter called Mary. Mr. Shopper was certainly a man who lived up to his name, because he absolutely loved shopping! He would shop every day of the year if he could, but his wife was not happy about this because as you can imagine, her house was *full* of the stuff he would buy. He had seven TVs in his room alone!

This story starts with Mr. Shopper getting up very early and making his kids' breakfast, before running out the door with about twenty shopping bags.

His eldest son, John tried to stop him, "Dad, where you going? It's Christmas..." but he didn't get the chance to finish, as his Dad was out of the door already, "... day!"

When Mr Shopper arrived in town, he was confused and thought to himself, what's going on? All the shops are closed? This was his worst nightmare come true.

"What's going on?" he asked to a man walking his dog nearby. "Why is everything closed?"

The man walking his dog looked at Mr Shopper like he had ten heads. "Why, it's Christmas Day Mr Shopper! You shouldn't be out shopping on Christmas Day. You should be at home spending it with your family."

Mr. Shopper stopped and thought while he looked at the twenty empty shopping bags in his hands. The man was right. The shopping could wait, and he wondered why he wanted to shop so much. He went back home, feeling a bit silly and said sorry to his family for running off on Christmas day, of all days.

Their Christmas day was great. Mr. Shopper's youngest son, Peter was excited because Santa had brought him a shiny red bike. Peter was so excited in fact, he didn't even realise that his Dad had gone out to the shops at all.

Mr Shopper said to Mrs Shopper as they watched Peter ride around, "Lucky the shops were closed today, I had my eye on five bikes just like the one that Santa brought to Peter."

"One is quite enough!" she joked.

After a huge Christmas dinner, Mr. Shopper suggested to his family that they play a boardgame. They all agreed, and Mr Shopper took his favourite boardgame from the pile, but you wouldn't believe what he'd chosen: 'The Shop-keeper's Dream'!

All his kids complained. "Ah Dad, please can we have one day where there is no mention of shopping?"

Mr Shopper was sad not to play the boardgame, but he did what his family wanted instead. He promised he wouldn't mention shopping for the rest of the day. And he didn't. They all had a great day watching Christmas movies and eating lots of tasty food.

But the next day, Mr. Shopper remembered it was St Stephens day, the day after Christmas and the sales were on in the shops.

His wife's brother was called Pat, and he owned an electrical shop on the main street in town. He did not like seeing Mr. Shopper coming. Once, Pat even put a 'closed' sign on the window to make Mr Shopper think he was closed, but this day the brother-in-law did not see him sneak in.

It only took Mr. Shopper two minutes to pile high five trolleys of goods. He had seven microwaves, eigh-teen toasters and six fridges and was looking for more when Pat saw him from the end of the aisle in the shop. He nearly fainted when he saw how much stuff he had in the trolleys. Pat couldn't let his brother-in-law buy this much from him, as he knew it was too much, even for Mr Shopper! It would be a waste of money. For Mr Shopper's own good, Pat threw him out of the shop and told him he was not allowed back. Ever. Mr. Shopper felt very sad.

One week later, the family kettle broke and Mrs. Shopper sent her husband to buy a new one from her brother, Pat's electrical store.

Maybe she needs *twelve* new kettles, Mr Shopper wondered to himself as he headed into town to buy the kettle. But he soon started to worry because Pat had said he could *never* come back into the shop again.

He came up with a plan. Before going to Pat's electrical shop, he went to the costume shop and bought a disguise. He was now wearing a fake moustache, a scruffy wig and a funny looking hat. He looked crazy!

As he walked into the electrical shop, Pat, his brother-in-law, did not recognise him at all and Mr Shopper thought he had got away with it. While he was back in the shop, he couldn't resist shopping! He went to the till with a basket full of ten kettles, all different colours.

Pat looked at this strange customer, thinking it bizarre for someone to buy ten kettles, but the man started to take them all out of his basket to be scanned.

Then a funny thing happened. A child came running down the centre of the store near the tills. Mr. Shopper was bending down to pick up the last kettle when the child knocked into him and the kettle fell out of his hands. The little messer, then grabbed Mr Shopper by the hair and the wig came off.

Pat shouted from the top of his voice: "Mr. Shopper, what are you doing here?!! You are barred from last week!"

Mr. Shopper had no intention of leaving quietly.

"What do you have against me, Pat? You know I love shopping! What's the harm? Can I at least have five kettles please? I love the colours of them!"

"No!" said the shop keeper firmly.

His shopping mania was so intense that a tussle ensued between them. Mr Shopper still wasn't leaving, and he held the five kettles tightly in his arms.

Pat threatened him. "You had better leave or I will have to call the guards! This is your final warning. If you don't get out of here now, I'm setting the law on you."

Mr. Shopper protested, "You wouldn't do that on family would you?"

Pat decided instead to ring his sister, Mr Shopper's wife. "You better get down here. Your husband is causing quite a scene. He has a trolley full of kettles and he won't let go of five of them. The other customers are getting very annoyed as there are no kettles left for anyone else!"

Mrs. Shopper said sorry to Pat and said she was on her way. She knew how to deal with Mr Shopper and his shopping habit.

When Mrs. Shopper got into the shop, her husband had added three phones to the trolleys also. Mrs. Shopper was cross. "What are you going to do with all this stuff?"

"But, we need a kettle, darling."

"I know, but we don't need all of them! Come on, put them all back and we will buy just one and go home again. Leave poor Pat and all his customers alone."

Mr. Shopper also had phones. "But I was going to get you a nice phone too. I couldn't make up my mind which was nicer so I thought I would get you three."

"One kettle is all we are buying!" she was serious.

Mr. Shopper eventually gave in and they left the shop with only what they needed, but not everything that Mr Shopper wanted. Poor Mr Shopper.

The End

Johnny No Shoes' Problems with Shoes

There once was a little boy called Johnny No Shoes. He was best friends with Larry Lamppost and they had lots of fun together. They went to the same school and hung out after school also. Now you might be wondering why he got the name Johnny No Shoes, well this is the story of why he has this name.

Johnny's parents had become sick and tired of buying Johnny shoes, because he simply could never find them! Every day he would go to school with the right shoe missing, or the left shoe missing, or odd mismatched shoes, or... as his names suggests: no shoes at all!

Johnny was always a quiet child and didn't have many friends. Larry though, was a very popular child. So let me tell you how this unlikely pair became the best of friends.

On Johnny's first day of school he came in wearing a Nike runner on the left foot and a Puma runner on the right foot. A bully named Nigel slagged poor Johnny all day about his mis-matched runners. Near the end of the day, Nigel tripped Johnny up as he was walking out of the classroom.

Larry had been getting very annoyed with Nigel all day, and when he tripped poor Johnny up, it was the last straw. Larry squared up to him.

"Hey, Nigel! What are you doing to poor Johnny? Don't you touch him again! Or you will have me to deal with!"

Being a bully, Nigel was used to making fun of people and having people laugh at his victims. No one ever pushed back, so he kept doing it. But he was afraid of Larry standing up to him. Nigel just stood there, stunned. All the class, including Larry and Johnny started to laugh at him. He could not take the tables turning against him and he ran away down the school corridor crying. No one could believe what they were seeing. Nigel was one of the toughest boys in the school, but he was reduced to tears.

"Thanks for sticking up for me." said Johnny to Larry. "I didn't know how to deal with him."

"No probs" said Larry, also adding, "Don't be afraid of him. Once you stand up to a bully and show you're not afraid, even if you are on the inside, bullies are not used to it and they are not as strong as they think."

Johnny agreed and started laughing. His laugh was unique and infectious, which made Larry want to laugh too. Larry liked being near Johnny's laughter and wanted to hang out with him. It was after this day that Larry and Johnny became the best of friends. Larry had started to call his new friend Johnny No Shoes, and Johnny liked this name as people would always ask, why are you called Johnny No Shoes? And they would tell this story.

They now help each other out with their issues. Mainly Larry and his issues with Lampposts, and Johnny and his issues with shoes… or no shoes! Johnny always tries to remember: if ever a bully tries to make fun of him, to not take the slagging or jeering to heart and don't let the words hurt you.

The End

The Story of Me-Me, Bop-Bop and Meehawl

Me-Me, Bop-Bop and Meehawl were good friends who loved hanging out together. Me-Me and Meehawl grew up in Dublin, but Bop-Bop grew up in the countryside of Hungary and moved over to Ireland a few years ago.

Ireland and Hungary were very different countries to grow up in, and times like birthdays, Christmases and Easters were very different in each country. Me-Me and Meehawl would tell Bop-Bop what they got for their birthday the Hungarian boy would sometimes be very surprised.

The first year that Bop-Bop was living in Ireland, Me-Me got a PlayStation for his birthday with the game, Donkey Kong.

Bop-Bop joked, "In Hungary we would get presents for our birthdays alright, but it would not be a PlayStation. One year we got a new donkey and played our own version of Donkey Kong!" They all laughed their heads off at the difference between the two countries.

Me-Me was a little messer in school. His teacher, Miss Orange would always blame him for everything that happened in the class. And most of the time she was right to! Today Miss Orange was teaching the class about healthy eating and she was asking the children to name foods that were good for them. Meehawl was the first to raise his hand.

"Yes Meehawl, what healthy food do you want to talk about?" asked the teacher.

"Fish, Miss!" replied Meehawl, with a grin.

"Good lad, Meehawl, and how is it healthy? When do you eat it?"

"Well me and my Ma and Da buy it in the chipper every Friday with loads of greasy chips and lots of salt and vinegar…" he added, "and a big bottle of Pepsi… yeah!"

The teacher was speechless while all the class fell around laughing. Miss Orange was getting angry and shouted at the class, "QUIET PLEASE!"

She continued, "Meehawl that is not a healthy way to eat fish. It's full of fat and grease and sugar, which are not healthy at all!"

"I know, but it's lovely-jubbly and tastes amazing!"

The teacher frowned and Meehawl could tell she was disappointed. "Ah Miss, I'm only messing."

Bop-Bop raised his hand and the teacher moved on from Meehawl.

"Yes, Bop-Bop, name a food you think is good for you." said Miss Orange, hoping for a sensible answer.

"In Hungary we are always very hungry, but now I'm starving listening to Meehawl's suggestion!"

The class laughed again. "Now, now, class! Come on. This is a serious topic. Has anyone any real ideas about eating healthy?"

There was no reply, so the teacher wrote a list of foods on the blackboard and asked the class to say which ones were good or bad for you. While she was doing that, she heard a funny noise coming from the back of the class... can you guess who it was? Me-Me had fallen asleep and was resting his head on the desk, snoring.

"Me-Me, wake up!" The teacher was furious.

"That's it! I'm ringing your parents!" shouted Miss Orange.

"You can't ring me Ma, she will be out." said Me-Me, knowing he would be in big trouble if his Ma found out.

"Well, you can't stay here in class if you're tired. Who can I ring to collect you?" insisted the teacher.

Me-Me didn't even need to think, he knew who would help him. "Well... me Uncle Tomo could come and get me, I guess?" Uncle Tomo was more like a friend than an uncle and Me-Me thought he was a great buzz.

Ring, ring... ring, ring... finally Uncle Tomo answered. "Hello, Uncle Tomo speaking..."

"Hello, Uncle Tomo, this is Miss Orange from Me-Me's school. I am Me-Me's teacher. Me-Me seems to be really, quite tired and is being disruptive in class today. Can you please come and collect him?"

Tomo replied, "Oh, I am sorry to hear that. Yes, I can be there in half an hour."

When Tomo came to collect him, Me-Me's eyes lit up because he knew that his Uncle would take him somewhere fun, and he did. They went to the coast in Bray, and then to the cinema and then McDonalds. Me-Me was so happy being with his Uncle Tomo.

After their adventure, Uncle Tomo was parking the car, when Me-Me saw Bop-Bop and Meehawl getting home from school because they all lived on the same road. He told them about his day out of school and asked them what they were doing.

"Just getting back from school." said Bop-Bop, he laughed, "That was so funny today with the healthy food lesson and you falling asleep!"

Meehawl was laughing too but felt bad inside, "I kinda feel sorry for winding up the teacher. I must say sorry tomorrow."

Uncle Tomo agreed and said with a big laugh, "The teacher has a load of children to deal with in the class. I couldn't do that job even if you paid me all the money in China!"

Me Me said to his uncle, "Why don't you bring me, Bops and Meehawl out tomorrow? It would be a great buzz!"

Uncle Tomo was put on the spot and left speechless for a second.

"Go on Uncle Tomo! You know you want to!" Me-Me continued.

His uncle hesitated and replied, "I can't tomorrow, Me-Me I am bringing my girlfriend, Susan on a date."

Me-Me teased his poor uncle, "Whoo, Susan!" and pretended to kiss an imaginary Susan.

Bop-Bop and Meehawl laughed as Uncle Tomo got embarrassed.

"Give it a rest Me-Me, you'll have a girlfriend one day. Anyway, I have to go now, see you lads around."

The next day Uncle Tomo collected his girlfriend from work and greeted her with a bunch of flowers. When Susan saw them she was shocked, in a nice way. "Wow!" she said. They're beautiful!" and she gave him a big kiss.

Across the road, Me-Me, Meehawl and Bop-Bop were going by Susan's work and saw everything.

"Hey, look over there. It's Tomo and Susan, the two love birds!" Me-Me said and went up to his uncle as the others followed. They said they were bored and asked if Tomo and Susan could take them to the coast again like yesterday.

Tomo replied, "Sorry lads, Susan and I are going for a surprise romantic meal later, so we can't bring you out today. We can do something another day though."

Upon hearing about this surprise meal, Susan told Tomo she loved him.

But Me-Me could not stop laughing and started slagging his uncle, teasing the couple, "I love you, I love you more, no, I love you more!" and started kissing and hugging an imaginary person. It caused poor Tomo and Susan to go as red as a strawberries and feel uncomfortable.

Although Me-Me just thought he was being funny around his uncle, who he knew very well, Meehawl felt uncomfortable for the couple too and spoke up, "Ah, leave them alone Me-Me. You shouldn't really be disturbing your poor uncle all the time anyway, after all, he is very good to you."

Me-Me thought for a second about what Meehawl had said and realised his friend was right.

"Ah, I'm only joking Uncle Tomo. You and Susan make a great couple, and hope you have a lovely meal. We'll leave you alone."

Uncle Tomo felt less embarrassed. 'Thanks Me-Me, that means a lot."

Me-Me, Bop-Bop and Meehawl made their way home and left Tomo and Susan to themselves. Although Me-Me and his uncle were very close and often slagged each other, it sometimes needs a friend to help point out when it's funny and when it's not.

The End

Wilma Wallpaper's New Hobby

This is the story of a little girl called Wilma Wallpaper, and guess what her favourite thing to do was? That's right, she loved wallpapering! Her enjoyment had started one Christmas when she got so excited she took every role of Christmas wallpaper she could find and covered the walls of her room with it. But she didn't just wallpaper the walls, she did the door, the window, her toys and even some clothes!

Mr and Mrs Wallpaper weren't happy about this. The paste was so thick on the door that it kept getting stuck in the door frame! They did see the funny side of it though when they saw the windows decorated in wallpaper and the light from outside coming through the images of Santa and reindeers and snowmen. But Wilma had used too much paste and it took ages to remove the wallpaper from the windows, and a lot of window cleaning to get it back to normal.

After her bedroom, Wilma also started to wallpaper other things, and other people even. One time Mary's Dad went to sleep on the couch and while he slept, she wrapped him in wallpaper from head to toe. When he woke the poor man couldn't move! He shouted, confused, "WILMA, I CAN'T MOVE! WHAT'S GOING ON?" Wilma couldn't stop laughing. She said sorry but thought he might like the colour. He found it hard to see a funny side to it as he removed the last of the paper from his jacket!

One of Wilma's favourite things to wallpaper was her bike. She would go everywhere on it and would constantly change the wallpaper it was covered in, which gave her friends a good laugh. Larry would ask her every month what wallpaper she was putting on her bike, and the answer would be something no one had thought of. One time she put pictures of Spain on her bike because that's where they went on holiday that year, but she had put too much wallpaper on the brakes and when she said Larry could have a go on her bike, he couldn't stop and crashed into a… well, you know what he crashed into by now, being Larry Lamppost!

One day all the children where in class and the teacher asked them to write a song or poem about their hobbies or favourite things to do. It didn't take Mary long to think of one, and she wrote a song about wallpapering, called 'Leave

Me Some Paper on the Wall'. All her friends thought the song was great, but also funny because only Wilma wallpaper could have written it.

Larry was learning guitar so he asked Wilma if he could put some music to her song. Wilma was very happy and excited by this and thanked Larry for his great idea, before wondering.

"Do you want me to wallpaper your guitar, Larry?" she asked.

"No way!" Larry replied, laughing. "My guitar is not to go anywhere near wallpaper!"

The teacher allowed Larry to bring his guitar to school the next day to practice. The thought of this was Larry's dream day at school because he would much prefer to be playing music than doing maths... ugh.

The next morning Larry was the first one in the house ready for school, which was very unusual for Larry as his dad would normally have to call him about a hundred times before he even moved.

"How come you are so excited about going to school today?" his dad asked.

Larry was excited. "The teacher is letting me bring my guitar to school today to put music to Mary's song."

"Who, Wilma Shopper?"

"No," said Larry, "Wilma Wallpaper."

His dad laughed, "Your have friends with funny names."

Larry was laughing too, "It's not like we have the most normal family name in the world, Dad!"

Mary was really excited too that day. She was at the school gate a whole hour before it opened.

The caretaker joked, "I must give you the key in future so you can open the school up!"

Mary replied, "I wouldn't do that, you know me and wallpaper! You wouldn't know what the place would look like! I've only been waiting here for a few minutes and think the school fence looks a lot better in this shade of red."

The caretaker looked at the bright red wallpaper now decorating a section of the school fence. He sighed. "Oh Wilma."

"Sorry," said Wilma, "I got bored."

"Better get this down before the principal arrives…"

Wilma and the caretaker got the last of it off just before the principal turned into the road towards the school.

Later that day the teacher announced what Larry and Wilma had been looking forward to all day. "At the end of this lesson, Larry and Wilma will perform their song for us all. Larry and Wilma you can go out and practice for a half an hour and come back and perform the song for the class."

Wow this is getting better by the minute, thought Larry. Getting time off class and practicing music!

The teacher warned, "No messing now children. And Wilma: no wallpapering!" The class chuckled.

"I won't, Miss, I promise."

And Larry and Wilma practiced. Wilma would sing the words first and then Larry would put some chords to it and it was coming together very nicely to the point they thought they had it finished.

The teacher came down the hall to get them. "Now children, are you ready to perform your song? The class are really excited to hear it!"

Wilma was getting nervous that maybe the song wasn't as good as she thought and there would be lots of pressure in front of the class.

Larry encouraged her. "Don't be silly, it's a great song, everyone is going to love it!"

The teacher suggested they play it just for her first and Wilma agreed and relaxed. They played it for the teacher who was very impressed. Wilma felt much better about herself after this because the teacher praised her and made her feel good about how she'd sung it.

They entered the classroom to play the song, and even though Wilma and Larry were a both a bit nervous, they overcame their nerves and performed the song as best they could, and they sounded great. Other classes overheard the song and started to come in and listen by the door. When they finished the song, there was a large round of applause which boosted Wilma and Larry's confidence sky-high.

The pupils and the teachers talked about the song for days and days afterwards. They were impressed with Larry's guitar skill and Wilma's voice. The song also helped people understand Wilma's love and fascination with wallpaper. Everybody likes different things. With Wilma, it was wallpaper.

Because it went so well, the teacher let Larry Lamppost bring his guitar to school once a month to make new songs with Wilma Wallpaper. Some of the other children in the class used this opportunity to see if they could get out of maths class, but the teacher did not even have to answer. The look on her face told the children the answer was a big NO!

Wilma's unusual habit with wallpaper didn't make her many friends, and a lot of bullies would bully her for being strange and different but because of her newfound talent for singing and writing music, anytime any of the bullies even dreamt of saying a bad thing about Wilma, they were soon put in their place by other children.

That's what the teacher really liked to see; to find the children' talent and make them shine and build their confidence. Wilma was so grateful to her teacher for helping her, she got her a nice thank you card, and at the end wrote: if you ever need any wallpapering done you know who to call.

Something happened to Wilma after this big turning point in her school life. She got into a new habit of writing songs and recording them with her friend, Larry. Because of this, she didn't wallpaper half as much as she used to. But had not stopped wallpapering completely. Just last week her parents came home to find the dog with funny wallpaper on his tail, but when asked how it got there Wilma admitted, "It's only his tail, at least I didn't wallpaper the whole of the dog!"

The End

Little Paddy Runner's Race Day

Little Paddy loved running ever since he was about five years old. At this age he would run in the playground in his school shoes, but when he started running around his local park in his school shoes, his mother warned him, "Your legs will be banjaxed if you run long distances in those shoes. You will get shin splints, and you don't want that!"

When he got his Dunnes Stores runners he was a happy little fella and ran even further distances. Once he ran 3 times around the park non-stop. He ran any time he could, after school, on weekends, on school holidays even.

When little Paddy was ten he started running with people who were a few years older than him. He ran with Brian often, who was in training for the Boston Marathon in America. Paddy wished he could do the Boston Marathon too, but Brian had said he was not ready and had to train for at least a year.

Paddy would go and watch the Dublin Marathon every year with his Dad and would think to himself afterwards that he could run for an entire marathon. You see, Paddy wasn't a very fast runner, but he had a great level of stamina, which meant he could run for a long time. He wished long distance running happened as a sport in school. He knew he would do well at that!

Then one day his chance came. There were entry-forms put up on the school noticeboard, inviting children to enter a country level five-kilometre race around Phoenix Park in Dublin and they would be representing his school, St Joseph's. It was open to all the kids in the school but only 6 children were brave enough to put their names down, and as you can imagine little Paddy was one of them.

The other 5 runners were all older than him and didn't think Paddy could win at all. Most of the children in his class did not support him either. They teased him by saying, "Why are you even doing this? You're too young and too slow! Paddy too-slow!" they laughed.

However, he did not listen to them. Believing in himself, Paddy knew that he was a good distance runner. The run was a month away and Paddy trained extra hard every day, right up to the day of the race.

He also told Brian about the race. Brian believed in Paddy and was happy to help him prepare and gave him great tips to follow. "Try to go slowly for the first kilometre," he advised, "before gradually picking up the pace." So they both practiced twice a week and did one extra day of just slow running. Brian's training really helped Paddy to prepare for the big day.

Saturday finally came. The day of the big race, and it was dry and sunny in Phoenix park. Paddy arrived early that morning and was warming up before everyone else. Over forty children were going to be taking part. When the rest of the students from his school turned up they could not believe their eyes when they saw Paddy jogging around the starting area and doing stretches. One or two even commented, "You're wasting your time Paddy, you're still going to be last!" followed by smart laughs and jokes. Paddy took no notice but kept on warming up, focusing on his own preparations and smiling to himself.

It was nearly eleven o'clock and the race was about to start. His teacher handed out all the kids representing St Joseph's their T-shirt, to show that they were part of the school team. Paddy was so proud as he put it on.

The race organiser got all the children in the race to the start line. Shouting "Ready… Steady…" he blew his whistle, and the race began. Everyone darted off as fast as they could, but Paddy took his time running at a steady pace, just like he'd practiced in the weeks building up.

Paddy was near the back of the pack, a good bit behind a lot of the other runners. His Mam and Dad were watching and encouraging Paddy, "Come on, run faster!" he could hear them cheer.

But he did not alter his speed, he had a game plan. He maintained his steady pace until the end of the first kilometre and then gradually increased his pace, overtaking three or four runners at a time who had started to become tired and had sore muscles. He even overtook his classmate, who just fifteen minutes ago had been laughing at him. This tactic was working a treat.

There were six children from his school taking part in the race and he was in second place in his school group as they reached the four-kilometre mark. He was in tenth place overall with a kilometre to go and still had stamina to keep up good pace and catch the runners in front. Things were going very well, but with only five-hundred metres to go, bad luck happened.

One of Paddy's laces opened up and he tripped up and fell! Thankfully he did not hurt himself badly, but did have a graze on his knee which was bleeding a bit. Some of the other runners ran past him and he was down to fifteenth place after he picked himself up again. He still had energy though and ran to the end of the race as fast as he could, managing to claw back some placed to finish in eighth place overall and second place within his school. He was so proud of himself, as was everyone else. What a great day for Paddy.

Two things happened after the race. Firstly, he was always picked first for all the games in the class, and he also got a medal from the school for his gutsy recovery performance. But the best thing Paddy got was the lesson that if there is something you truly love to do, keep it up and enjoy it and you will do well.

The End.

Jet's Tale

This is a story about a little girl called Kate, whose Dad owned a racehorse called Jet. Jet was Kate's favourite horse in the whole world and she often looked after her in the stud farm where the horse was trained.

You see, Jet was a very successful racehorse and would often win big races. Kate's Dad was also the trainer and spent a lot of time with Jet, getting her ready for races, training, feeding and transporting her around the country. Every weekend Kate's Dad would allow Kate to help on the stud farm and Kate loved to take Jet out on Saturday mornings, jumping over the training fences in the field they owned.

The stud farm was large and was next to their large country home. Jet was the most successful horse they had and a successful racehorse generated a lot of money for its owners.

Kate would always go to the races and be cheering Jet on to win, which she quite often did. One day, she was at a racecourse in Dublin called Leopardstown, a local race not far away from the family home. Jet was in the biggest race of the day and was leading with just a few furlongs to go. But then disaster struck.

Jet caught her leg in the final fence and fell. Thankfully the jockey was ok, but poor Jet crashed to the ground and was really hurt. Kate really wanted to get to her and her Dad had to hold her back from running onto the course. The officials and the vets had to assess the injury and the best way to help.

After the vet had checked Jet over, it was clear that it would be a long while before Jet would be back racing again. Kate spent most of her time in the stable, happy to help and care for Jet as she recovered.

Things got tough for Kate's family after the accident. They relied upon Jet ability to race and win in order to keep the finances going in the household. It took a while for Kate to adjust to not having all the big days out and all the nice things she was used to getting, but Jet recovery was her most important focus.

Thankfully, Jet did recover and was able to race again. It took a while to get up to her usual flying speed, but when she did, she was back winning races again; and even more than she used to!.

Over the next few years, Jet won three quarters of the races she entered, which was a record in Irish horse racing.

But then Jet had to stop racing because she was going to have a little baby foal. Kate, as you can imagine, was so excited.

The foal was born and it was a boy horse. His skin was snow white, so they called him Snowy. Kate loved to feed Snowy apples and carrots and he was very calm around humans and would eat them out of her hand. This made Kate really happy. She spoke to Jet and thanked her. "Thank you so much, Jet, I love Snowy." Now horses can't talk, but Kate knew from the look in Jet eye that she loved her young foal too. Snowy was destined to become a race horse like his mother.

Kate loved looking after Jet and Snowy. She knew this was exactly what she wanted to do for a living when she was older.

Kate wanted her friends to be able to join her when taking out the horses, but race-horses needed to be trained and lean, so she kept pestering her Dad for a gentle, social horse that could be ridden by her and to teach her friends how to ride on. The new horse had the smallest nose she had ever seen. Kate's two best friends were called Billy and Barry, so she named the new horse Billy Barry Small Nose!

Kate brought her friends from school to her house and would teach them how to ride Billy Barry Small Nose, which made her a very popular girl in school. When Kate went into secondary school she made a little business for herself, advertising horse-riding lessons to any students who were interested. And many were. It was the start of a hugely successful passion, and made her Mam and Dad very proud.

But Kate knew it was Jet that started her passion with horse riding, and Jet would always have a large place in her heart for the rest of her life.

The End.

Fefe, Lally & Ballie's Day Trip to the Zoo

This story starts with a little boy call Fefe and a little girl called Lally, who were next door neighbours and they loved playing in their back gardens! Any time Fefe was out playing and heard Lally in her garden, he would ask his Dad if he could join her. And Lally did the exact same when she heard Fefe playing in his back garden. Both were so happy to have such a good friend living next door.

One day Fefe was jumping on his trampoline and Lally noticed. She asked her Dad "Daddy, Fefe is on the trampoline. Can I jump, too, pleeeeease!"

Lally's Dad saw no harm, "Of course, if Fefe's Dad says it's ok."

Fefe's Dad gave him an ice cream and Lally shouted to her Dad over the fence, "Daddy, Fefe's got an ice cream. Can I have one, too, pleeeease!"

It always went like this. Every time they played together they wanted what the other one had. Their Dads chuckled about their two kids wanting the same things all the time.

Lally and Fefe always left their windows open when they were going into their beds. They wanted to make sure they were told the same bedtime story, given the same drink, at the same time. When the weather was bad and they had to close the window, they used walkie talkies just to make sure they were each getting the same!

One day the Fefe and his Dad, along with Lally and her Dad all decided to go to the zoo together. They decided to take a picnic and the kids made sandwiches with potato crisps and their Dads told the kids to pack plenty of fruit in the basket too.

Fefe and Lally were so happy to be heading to the zoo together. The weather was amazing and when they got in the gates Fefe was saying to his Dad "I want to see the monkeys!" and Lally was saying to her Dad "I want to see the giraffes!" Fefe's Dad suggested they split up so Fefe will see the monkeys and Lally and her Dad can see the giraffes. Then they would meet for a picnic in a while, but Fefe and Lally both said at the same time, "Nooooo! We want to go and see everything together!"

The monkeys were closer, so they all went to see the monkeys first and then the giraffes.

Fefe was eating a bag of cheese and onion crisps when they got to the monkey enclosure. They were looking at a big monkey high up in one of the trees when suddenly a small baby monkey jumped down from another perch and put his hand through the bars and stole Fefe's potato snacks! Poor Fefe was very upset. Lally being such a good friend shared her crisps with him and that made him feel much better.

Lally joked, "We better eat the crisps before we go to see the giraffes because we hear they can be very hungry!"

They were gradually getting to see all the animals. "This is the best day ever!" the kids said.

When they got to the playground. Fefe wanted to play on the monkey bars, and you can guess what Lally wanted to do! Fefe now found it so funny that the funny monkey stole his crisps.

Everyone was feeling hungry so they decided to have their picnic in the grass near the playground. They found a nice sunny spot to put down their picnic blanket and the kids tucked into their crisp sandwiches straight away. Next thing they heard a shout, "Fefe, Lally how are youse?" It was their other friend, Ballie and he ran over to them.

Ballie was their friend, but he could be a little messer at times. He ran over and took one of Lally's sandwiches and also stole the bobble from her hair. He started demanding of Fefe's Dad, "Where's my sandwich, I want a sandwich too!"

Fefe and Lally's Dads were not happy one bit with Ballie. "Stop being bold to Lally and give back her bobble!

Where are your Mammy and Daddy, Ballie?" They looked over and Ballie's Dad was fast asleep. On the grass a roaming peacock was pecking at Ballie's lunch.

Lally's Dad went over and woke Ballie's Dad, explaining that Ballie was being very bold. Ballie's Dad said he was very sorry for the way his son was going on and threatened to Ballie, "if you keep being bold we are going to go home!"

Ballie said sorry to everyone, but he looked really sad because all his lunch was gone. They all felt sorry for Balllie and his Dad and shared what was left of their picnic with them.

You might remember from earlier in the story, that Fefe and Lally's Dads asked them to bring some fruit for the picnic. Wow, did they bring fruit! They brought twenty bananas each, seventeen apples and twenty-four oranges! The Dads all laughed when they saw the amount of fruit! Ballie made a lot of it disappear very fast.

When they finished the picnic, Ballie started acting up again and shouted demandingly at Fefe's Dad, "I want chips. Now!"

It was the last straw for Ballie's Dad, "Right. That's it we are going home, young man!" He took him home, apologising for his son's behaviour.

It was getting late anyway and Fefe and Lally were wrecked, saying that they were very tired and they had seen all the animals, so they all set off for home too. Fefe and

Lally thanked their Dads for such a great day and slept in the car all the way home.

When they got home, Fefe's Mammy was preparing a nice dinner and she invited Lally to stay for dinner too. Lally's dad said it was fine. They were about to tuck into their yummy yum yums when the doorbell went. Fefe's Mam went to answer it.

It was Ballie again! He said that his Mam and Dad said he was allowed to play with Fefe and Lally for a while before bed time. He walked straight in, being rude to Fefe's Mam right from the start. "Where's my dinner? I want it now!"

Fefe's parents were speechless, and they rang Ballie's house. Ballie's Dad answered and was very apologetic, "Oh! I'm very sorry. I thought he was up in his room. He must have sneaked out. I will be over to get him right away!"

Ballie's Dad got to Fefe's house and told Ballie to apologise for being so rude. "If you keep going on like this, you won't be allowed play with Fefe and Lally anymore!"

Ballie cried. He didn't want that. "You're right Dad. I love you too. I'm sorry."

Ballie went home with his Dad and was very sorry to Fefe's parents for his carry on. Fefe and Lally had their dinner and played for half an hour before bed time.

The next morning Lally called for Fefe after breakfast and suggested they surprise Ballie and call for him. Ballie was playing ball on his own in his garden and when Fefe and Lally called he was so happy to see them. He now had someone to play with.

Ballie's Dad was happy to see the three kids paying nicely and asked them if they wanted to come to the amusements in Bray with him and Ballie. "Oh yes! Please!" Fefe and Lally said, "but we need to ask our Mams and Dads first." They ran home and asked. Their parents said yes and gave them a tenner each to spend in the amusements. This was turning out to be a great day!

They got the train to Bray and had great fun playing "I Spy" and "Yes and No" games. When they got there, they went for a nice walk along the seaside. Fefe and Lally were happy enough with the walk for the moment when Ballie started shouting at his Dad.

"I want chips! I want chips! Get me chips. Now!" Fefe and Lally didn't know why he was acting like this.

His Dad replied, "Ballie, come here and give me a hug."

Ballie changed his tone and said he was sorry. "I promise I will be good after you get me chips."

Fefe and Lally were thinking our Mam's and Dads wouldn't get us chips if we went on like this, but Ballie's Dad gave in and got them some chips and Ballie was good again.

Then they went to the amusements where Fefe and Lally played for ages on the basketball game which they loved. Fefe won five games to four. Then Ballie got to play the winner of the game, and played air hockey with his dad while he waited.

Ballie wanted to win a Playstation. There was a claw machine that gabbed the prizes which offered a Playstation as the top prize, in the fun fair. His poor Dad had already spent about twenty euro trying to win it. He had to try guide the claw and pick up the prize.

Ballie pleaded "Please just one more try. It's only a euro. Just one more. Pleeease" His Dad had one more go and the kids couldn't believe what happened next. His Dad won the Playstation! Ballie was so happy. What a great end to the day.

That Summer was so much fun for the three friends. Their Mams and Dads took turns in taking them to different places.

The two kids' parents were good friends as well as neighbours and they decided to put the children in the same school, which as you can imagine, made Fefe and Lally really happy.

That first morning the kids awoke really early at 5.00 a.m. They were so excited about going to school. Fefe and Lally were talking via the walkie-talkie and raced into their parent's bedrooms all excited, shouting "Come on Mam and Dad, get up, get up. You have to get me ready for school, I want to play with me friends!"

When they arrived at the playschool the Mammy's and Daddy's had tears in their eyes saying goodbye to their little messers for the first time. Then the teacher arrived. Her name was Ms. Apple Cake.

The children were waiting to go in and all said in unison, "Good morning Ms. Apple Cake."

Fefe and Lally found it hard not to laugh at the teacher being called Ms Apple Cake. It was their favourite dessert. Then Lally said to Fefe, "Lucky Ballie isn't here would probably shout that he wants apple cake!"

Then guess who showed up? Ballie and his Daddy! They arrived lightly late, but just in time to hear the chorus of the children saying 'good morning Ms Apple Cake' at the front door.

His poor Dad looked like he hadn't had a wink of sleep and even though Ballie heard all the children saying good morning Ms. Apple Cake, he surprisingly didn't say anything apple or cake related!

The new school children went into the classroom together and were shown around the toys and met all their class mates.

Once Lally got in she started to cry, but Ms Apple Cake was a nice lady and helped her settle in. Fefe was there too, and they did some painting and Lego and then she was fine.

About an hour passed and the children were all happy. Then they met another teacher whose name was Ms Ice-Cream! That's when Ballie started.

"I WANT APPLE PIE AND ICE-CREAM NOW!"

Fefe and Lally tried to help the teacher, "Ballie you can't shout that at the teachers. That's just their names." but it didn't help, and he kept shouting.

Ballie was less than an hour and a half in playschool before Ms. Apple Cake had to send him to the bold step. If the bold step didn't stop him shouting she would have to ring his parents.

On the bold step, Ballie was on his own and learned that shouting would not get him what he wanted. And within ten minutes he wanted to be back in the classroom playing, so stopped shouting. He was as good as gold again. Fefe and Lally were surprised.

Later that day, all the children got apple cake and ice-cream for dessert anyway, so the thing to remember from this story is that by shouting all the time you might get what you want for a short time, but people will not always be able to give you what you want. If you are kind and patient, good things happen, and you might even get that ice-cream anyway.

The End

Johnny No Shoes Meets Mr. Shopper and his Daughter Mary

One day Mr. Shopper was in town looking for a new pair of shoes for his daughter, Mary. Or rather 12 new pairs of shoes, being Mr Shopper!

Johnny No Shoes was in the same shoe shop with his Dad. Hopefully they could find a pair of shoes that he might not lose for once. Johnny's Dad was asking the shop assistant whether there were any shoes that were hard to fall off, and he explained about his son who keeps losing his.

The shop assistant looked puzzled by the question when Mr. Shopper butted in. "What I do is, just buy a few pairs at once."

Johnny looked into Mr. Shopper's trolley with shock. There weren't just a few pairs in there, there were about forty!

Mary's face went red with embarrassment when she saw Johnny No Shoes seeing her Dad's shopping trolley over flowing with shoes. Johnny was in the same school as her, but he didn't tease her and instead they laughed about it.

Johnny and his Dad ended up getting a pair of shoes with 'special-non-fall-off-grip' technology, which didn't make much sense to anyone, but given how much Johnny loses shoes, anything was worth a try!

Mr. Shopper reassured, "I bought fifty pairs of those shoes for my son and I'm nearly sure he still has them all!" Then he had a moment of doubt. "On second thought, I must get a few more pairs."

Before Mr Shopper could put yet more shoes in the trolley, Mary stopped him. "No Dad! He doesn't need them! Let's just buy what we have and leave." And that's exactly what they did. They said goodbye to Johnny and his Dad.

Mary and Johnny went to the same school, but didn't really know each other well until the shoe shop incident. They had a good laugh about the day before in the shop and Johnny said to Mary that he liked his new special-non-fall-off-grip shoes! "Everyone is surprised in my class, that I have matching shoes for once!"

Mary thought they looked cool on Johnny. She said with a laugh, "They should call you Johnny cool shoes now!"

Johnny was very happy he made friends with Mary. He suggested she should call for him and she could hang out with him and his good friend Larry Lamppost.

Mary laughed, "I love your friend's second name, Lamppost."

Johnny replied, "It's a great name isn't it? Larry is so nice you will get on well with him."

It turned out that Mary didn't live too far away from the lads and they ended up all becoming good friends. One day they were all talking about their names, and Johnny asked Mary, "You know the way your second name is Shopper, do you take after your Dad when you go to the shops?"

Mary defended, "No way!" but added, "Well, not any-more I guess is more correct. When I was younger and went to the toyshop, I saw Barbie dolls and I wanted every single one in the shop and that's why my Mam would always bring me. She wouldn't let my Dad go with me, because she knows what he's like! You can guess who I wanted to go with though!"

Mary asked Johnny about his surname, No Shoes, and how his problems with losing shoes started. She looked down at his ...oh no! ... his bare feet!

Johnny explained, "My Dad says that it started when I was very small. I could never really hold on to any of my shoes or keep track where they were when I took them off. I would lose all shoes, even the ones that cost the most, which my dad was always mad at! As you can see the situation hasn't got much better," he gestured his bare feet, "I just lost my favourite pair of NIKE runners!"

They all saw the funny side of it though. Oh poor Johnny…

Mary asked Larry about his second name. "What about you, when did your issues with lampposts start?"

Larry told her, "It's a long story. As far back as I can remember I have always had mishaps with lampposts. Sometimes when I was really tired, I would always find myself running or walking smack-bam into lampposts and my brothers would always slag me about it!"

They all laughed.

"Tell her about Peter." said Johnny.

"Lamppost accidents actually run in the family," said Larry, "we all have our problems with lampposts, like my brother, Peter. We get on the best now, but he used to slag me about it the most! A few years back I was coming home from school and saw him on his skateboard so called over to say hello. He wasn't looking where he was going and crashed into a lamppost! He thought I was going to tell my other brothers and make fun of him like he did me all the time, but I was more worried whether he was ok. He promised he would stop slagging me about lampposts if I didn't tell the rest of my brothers what happened!"

"That's a good story, Larry." said Mary, with a big grin on her face.

Johnny added, "It's funny that our surnames perfectly suit us!"

They all agreed, but this subject would become a lot more meaningful the very next day.

They were all in school and the teacher announced their next class project. "Now class, I want you to write a story about one of your friends and their surname and where it came from. There will be prizes for the best story!"

Larry and Johnny were smiling from ear to ear thinking, this should be fun. After school that day the lads went for a game of pool near where they lived and Johnny asked Larry, "Who are you going to write about?"

"I have a few people in mind." He took his shot, potting a red ball.

"Me too." said Johnny.

They both agreed that Mary's surname would be funny to write about.

"We would have to find out where the name came from."

Johnny laughed, "Could we not just say it came from Tesco or something?"

Mary didn't give anything away in school, but the story she was thinking of writing was on the surname, Lamppost. She called Larry's Dad on the phone that evening and said she was writing a story for school and she wanted to do it on their family name.

Larry's Dad found this very unusual and was quiet for a few moments. He wasn't really sure what to say, but knew a bit about his family history, so invited Mary over to his house. "You had better bring a pen and paper!" he said.

When Mary arrived, Larry's Dad was ready and had prepared some old photos to show. He asked asked how long the story was going to be.

Mary said it would just a few paragraphs about their family name.

So off he went with his story, "My great-grandfather was involved in the lighting industry after the First World War. He was living in Poland at the time and as you can imagine there wasn't many streetlights left after the war!" He asked, "Are you learning about the First World War in school at the moment Mary?"

Mary nodded.

"He supplied most of Poland with candle lit lampposts which made him very popular indeed. His name was Barry John Long Lamppost." said Mr. Lamppost with a chuckle.

Mary thought this name was funny and tried not to laugh in front of Larry's Dad, but was sure this would make her story a funny one for the class and win her the teacher's prize.

Mr Lamppost had been talking and showing photos for what felt like ages to Mary. She looked at the clock on the wall and was a bit bored, but Mr Lamppost would not stop talking!

"…and that's when we realised the lampposts would be better with electricity…" He paused.

Mary jumped on the pause. "Thanks a million Mr. Lamppost, this is a great story and I think I have enough now. Besides, I really need to head home for my dinner."

Mr Lamppost still had loads to say, but it was getting late. "Oh, ok, no problem Mary, thank you for being so interested and good luck with the story."

It came to the day that the stories had to be read out and they were all very excited. The teacher was finishing her English lesson and said to the class, "Ok, here is the moment you have all being waiting for, the story competition, so who wants to go first?"

None of the class volunteered, instead they were all quiet, none wanting to be the first to stand up. The teacher joked, "I must do this more often I have never seen you guys so quiet and well behaved!" The teacher waited for a few minutes, and then decided to pick someone.

"Mary Shopper, would you mind going first?"

Nigel the bully didn't help her nerves, "I bet it's rubbish!"

Larry stuck up for her, "At least she CAN write, bet you haven't even written anything!"

The teacher wanted to make an example of Nigel. "Well Nigel, if you're being so smart let me hear your story first."

Nigel went red. "Oh sorry Ms. I had my story written, it was really good, but my dog ate it!"

All the class broke out laughing at Nigel. They all knew he was lying and the teacher sent him to the headmaster.

Mary got up and told her story about Larry's surname and his great, great grandfather, Barry John Long Lamppost and all the class loved it and applauded and the end.

"Fair play Mary" said Larry, "but then my Dad has some imagination and can go on a bit!" He couldn't believe Mary even had photos to back up his Dad's story.

Larry got up next and told his story about Mary Shopper's Granny and explained how her love of shopping began. She was very wealthy and lived in a big big house in the country and fell in love with shopping. Mary's Dad grew up having everything! They had a swimming pool in the back of the house, a gym and Mary's favourite place to visit; the games room.

All the class, including Johnny, thought Mary was very lucky!

One-by-one each student got up and told the story they had written until all of them were done.

The teacher then asked Johnny.

"What story have you written?"

"Sorry Miss, I haven't finish mine yet!"

Then Nigel shouted out.

"JOHNNY NO STORY!"

The teacher went easy on him saying.

"Can you have it in next week please Johnny!"

"Thanks Miss, I will I promise!"

"All the stories that were told today are brilliant," the teacher said, "it's going to be so hard to pick a winner!" Just then, the lunch bell went. The teacher said she would pick the winners and give out the prizes after lunch break. None of the children even wanted to go to lunch, they were so excited!

After lunch the children were still excited and it took them a while to quieten down, but in time they did, and the teacher began.

"All your stories have been excellent. You should all be very proud of yourselves, please give yourselves a round of applause." All the class clapped, and the teacher continued, "But there has to be a winner. I have prizes for first, second and third place and I award third place, first." The excitement in the class increased.

"In third place we have Wilma Wallpaper who wrote a great story about Daisy Murphy's great grandmother, who was a survivor on the Titanic." The class clapped Wilma Wallpaper. "Well done Wilma, you have won a homework pass for a whole month!" She was so happy with this as no one liked doing homework!

"Second prize goes to Larry Lamppost for your great story about Mary Shopper's Grandmother and her big house and spending habits!" The class applauded again. "You have won cinema vouchers for you and a friend." Larry was chuffed, he was happy he put the work in now!

Then the teacher announced the overall winner, "And finally, let's hear it for our overall winner today, Mary

Shopper and her story about Barry John Long Lamppost!" All the class were very happy for her and applauded the loudest. She even got a cheer from Nigel the bully, who was now back in the class and behaving a bit better.

For her prize, Mary won a month pass for four friends for the cinema which made her very popular in the class! She said to Larry and Johnny, "I will bring you guys first, for definite." The lads said thanks and they all wondered what film they wanted to go and see.

Mary, Larry and Johnny often talked and joked about the stories they had written for that competition. Larry laughed his head off when Mary told him that she got all the details direct from his Dad. Mr Lamppost's stories were the longest! Mary had said it was fair play to Mr Lamppost, after all he got them all a good few outings to the cinema!

That's nearly the end of this story, except to say that none of this would have ever happened without good friends. Making good friends can sometime be instant over a chance meeting or sometimes take time over lots of shared experiences, but once you have them, they are the most important thing. Friends can help each other out, laugh together, cry together, and will be there for you if you need them. Part of being a friend is to be there for them if they need you too. So yes, indeed; friendship is worth more than a pot of gold.

The End

Fefe, Lally & Ballie's Halloween

Fefe, Lally and Ballie were all five years old and in senior infants. It was that scary time of year again known as Halloween and was the last day of school before they got their holidays. The teacher had arranged a Halloween party for all the class where they all had to dress up as something scary! Lally was dressed up as a witch, Fefe as a ghost and Ballie was a pumpkin. The teacher was very impressed with the children's efforts.

Fefe kept hiding from the others then jumping out and shouting Boo! All the class were laughing their heads off, but after an hour or so of this, the teacher became unhappy. She said "Now, Fefe it's time to sit down and be good please, or you will have to sit on the bold step." Fefe eventually sat down before Ballie started running around shouting, "I'm a scary pumpkin raaaaarrrr!", which set the whole class wild again.

The poor teacher was trying to organise a last day of school talent show where the children could impress their friends by doing something entertaining for the rest of the class. She said "Everyone sit down please and we can talk about the prizes for today!"

And wow did that work, they all sat down as quite as mice.

The teacher continued, "We are going to have a talent show for the last day of school."

Fefe shouted, "I want to sing! I love singing! Please Ms can I sing?"

Meanwhile Lally was thinking she would do a dance, she loved dancing.

Ballie was going to tell a joke in front of the class.

As you would imagine, all the kids were really happy to hear there was a talent show and they all wanted to do the thing they loved.

So Fefe sang a song called 'Monster Mash' and it went down a treat with the other children in the class. He did all the actions with it and was so happy with himself.

Then it was Lally's turn. The teacher asked her what she was going to do and she said she wanted to dance to a song. "What song do you want to dance to, love?"

"I don't know. I feel very shy." said Lally, red-faced, 'Please don't call me love.'

The teacher encouraged, "You will be great, Lally! I will even dance with you if you like?" Lally jumped up and said she wanted to dance to Michael Jackson's song, 'Thriller'.

So the teacher played the song on the music system and Lally and the teacher started dancing to the song and the rest of the class joined in. They all had so much fun dressed up and scary monsters, ghosts and ghouls!

Soon it was Ballie's turn and the teacher asked him what he wanted to do for the talent show.

Ballie said confidently, "I'm going to tell a joke. It's a scary joke for Halloween. What did one ghost say to the other ghost when he was telling a fib?"

All the class replied, "We don't know…"

"You're lying, I can see right throuuuuugh you!"

The kids and the teacher, laughed, thinking it was very funny. They all clapped afterwards.

All the class had so much fun that day in school. When it was time to go home they even asked the teacher if they could they stay for longer!

The teacher said some last words before their parents came to take the children home. "I just want to say a very well done to all the class today, all your singing, dancing and joke-telling was amazing. I hope you have a great Halloween holiday, and don't forget, be very, very careful around bonfires and please don't go near fireworks because they are so dangerous!"

The class all nodded and agreed, and then they were on their holidays for a whole week.

Later that evening Fefe, Lally and Ballie were very excited to be going out, trick-or-treating for Halloween, where they would knock on people in their street for sweets and chocolate. They all met up outside Fefe's house carrying the biggest bags they could find in their houses. Soon they hoped their bags would be full of chocolate, jellies, bars, and all things nice!

They knocked on all the houses in the area and came away with lots of treats. They got to one particular house, that looked very spooky with lots of scary ornaments in the garden; pumpkins carved as scary monsters, skeletons, witches, spider webs and ghosts. Lally and Ballie where scared, saying there was no way they were knocking on this house.

Fefe was not scared a bit, though. "It's only decorated for Halloween," he said, "it's not real! I'm going in anyway. It means more sweets for me!"

Fefe walked past all the scary things in the front garden, and went up the door and pressed the doorbell, which emitted sounds of blood-curdling screams and scary laughter. He had second thoughts at this stage, and became a bit scared himself. The person answered the door dressed as Frankenstein and Fefe jumped back.

The man said in a deep, scary voice, "what do you want child!?"

Fefe asked in a shivery voice, "Hello sir, t..t.. trick or treat! Can you help the Halloween party please?" he gestured to his bag of sweets.

The man started to laugh and some of the scariness went away. "Of course!" he said, and filled Fefe's bag to the top. "That's for being so brave!"

When Lally and Ballie saw what happened they got the courage to run past the scary garden up to the front door for treats too. It was scary, but so fun to get lots of treats. They would have enough treats to last them all month after this evening! Eventually, and after knocking on lots of houses, all the children decided to finish their trick-or-treating.

They all went to Fefe's house where his Mam and Dad had dressed up as vampires and organised a Halloween party for them. His Mam played all the best Halloween scary songs and they danced and sang to The Monster Mash and Thriller. There was so much chocolate and sweets stashed in the children's bags, and they piled it all out on the table to count. Fefe's Mam and Dad couldn't even see the table because there was so much they'd collected!

When the party was over, they shared out all the sweets they'd got, and Lally and Ballie got ready to go home. Fefe's Mam warned them both, "don't eat all of your sweets in one go now, or you will be very sick!" They said they wouldn't, but they certainly wanted to! They said Happy Halloween to Fefe and then headed home.

Before each of the children fell asleep that night they said to their parents, that it was the best Halloween night ever. We can't wait for next Hallowee... They didn't even finish their sentence, and fell fast asleep... like Halloween zombies!

The End

Stephen Little's School Days

This story began more than forty years ago, back in 1980. Stephen was a four-year old boy starting school. He was a very small little boy who, like any other child of his age was brought to the school by his Mammy. On the very first day he was in the class only a few minutes before running straight back out after his Mam. Somehow, he knew he was not going to like school, even at such an early age.

After a few days of this, and after a fair few tears had been shed, his Mammy stayed in the playground for a bit longer after dropping him off and made sure little Stephen was OK before leaving. This helped, and Stephen started to settle in more and would play with the other children in his junior infant's class. He made some friends called Stewart and another one called Fergus. Fergus was even shorter than little Stephen! They played together for the rest of that year, and school became a little easier for Stephen with friends.

The next year when they started senior infants and were that bit taller and braver, Stewart and Stephen were still friends and were playing in the yard at break when Stewart challenged to Stephen, "Do you want to run away from the school for a laugh?"

Stephen agreed to the challenge. They knew they shouldn't do it, but it seemed fun at the time. So they ran to the school gate, unnoticed by the teachers among all the other children playing, and both ran off down the road.

There was panic in the school as teachers and pupils all searched for the two boys missing from class role call! Luckily, a lady was walking into her house when she saw the two little kids with their uniforms on and phoned the school. They were only a few hundred yards from the grounds, but the lady marched them back to the main gate. A sight to which everyone was happy. And guess what they were doing when they got back? Each munching on a Twix bar! That is when Stephens's life-long love of Twix bars began.

As the senior infants moved into primary school, Stephen was kept back a year and had to say goodbye to a lot of the friends he'd made after first class as they moved on. He was a step behind the rest of the class with many subjects, and although he didn't want stay back a year at the time, he ended up making one or two good friends in the new class, who would end up remaining friends with him all the way through his primary school years.

I was not all plain sailing for little Stephen growing up though primary school and he encountered a lot of bullying throughout these years. He was terrified of fighting, and it showed. All the bullies could sense this fear and made life very hard for the poor lad. They would sometimes steal his lunch, and if he hadn't bought lunch yet, they would sometimes steal his lunch money instead. What made it worse it was the money that his Mam worked hard to give him each day. The teachers were not much help either. He would try and tell them what happened, but they wouldn't do much about it apart from saying to ignore the problem.

That was the bad side of Stephen's childhood, but there were good memories too. In the holidays his Dad would bring him to Blackpool in the UK every summer, which was great fun, and often, he would also bring him and his sister on a day ticket to travel around Dublin on the train all day. They would end up riding the train down to Bray for fish and chips, followed by a spin on the amusements. Stephen's big talent was singing, and he was never shy to perform in front of anyone and everyone, so after fish and chips they would sometime go into a pub where Stephen would sing his little lungs out. He loved spending this time with his Dad, who always made their time together full of fun and laughter.

When Stephen was in fourth class his teacher announced that the RTE TV station was coming into the school to film a programme called "Party Pieces". The programme involved children being auditioned for the show where they would get the chance to sing on TV; it was like a very early version of "Ireland's Got Talent". You can guess that Stephen auditioned, and he certainly did, along with a few of his friends. The experience for him would be like all of his Christmases coming at once! It was also a brilliant break from the everyday misery of the bullying. He sang the Bon Jovi song, "Living on a Prayer" and the piano player from RTE played along with the song. As he sung away, he was thinking to himself, "Wow!! What a moment!!"

It took a few weeks for the TV judges to come back and say who'd got chosen for the show. On that day, Stephen was sitting in class trying to work out his sums when the crackly school intercom came on with a "Bing-Bong" noise.

The principle, Sister Vera, loudly made an announcement: "CHILDREN AND TEACHERS, YOUR ATTENTION PLEASE..."

The announcement nearly blew the ears off the class it was so loud!

The principle continued, "...Can the following children please make your way to room 7. You have been chosen for the RTE Party Pieces programme..."

When the sister called out little Stephen's name, he could not believe it. His fellow classmates began clapping their hands in recognition. It was one of the proudest moments for someone who was being constantly picked on by the bullies in his class. Being cheered by everyone, he wanted the moment to last forever.

Stephen's friend Anthony had also auditioned, singing a song called "They say that in the Army", but did not get picked to come to room 7. Stephen really felt for Anthony, but Anthony was still happy for Stephen. That is the way friends should be after all.

When Stephen went and performed his song in front of the camaras, he felt like a little rockstar; if only for that one hour, but he had to wait for nearly a whole year to pass before the programme came on the telly. And when it did finally show, he was so let down as his performance didn't make the broadcast. To make the disappointment ten times worse, he had told everyone about his upcoming moment on TV and they all tuned in expecting to see him. It was a tough experience, but Stephen did not get overly put off by it, such was his love for singing. He was happy for the friends in his class that did get their performances shown.

As well as the close brush with performing, school also generated funny times. Stephen and his friend, Anthony went for extra help with reading two days a week with a nun called Sister Sheila, whose mood would change depending on the day of the week. Her mood wouldn't be just slightly different, she would be like a different person!

The boys went to her on Tuesdays and Thursdays. On a Tuesday, she was the holiest, sweetest nun in the world. She would love to help Stephen and Anthony with their reading, and encouraged the two boys to do well, sometimes even giving the boys treats. But on a Thursday, well; she was a different nun altogether. If Stephen or his friend got even one word wrong in the book, she would poke them with a red pen. At the end of the class on a Thursday they would both have more red ink on their hands than on the page! They got very used to this pattern over the years of going to her.

On Stephen's last day of sixth class, they had an end of year party in the class-room. It was a Friday afternoon and Stephen and Anthony were both full of sugar and giggles when they happened to be passing Sister Sheila's reading room. They walked in to say goodbye to her and thankfully she was having one of her 'good' days.

When they walked in, the reading teacher was vacuuming the classroom and she asked the two sugar-filled friends to help, which they did. But Anthony had another idea up his sleeve. While the nun was hoovering the floor, he removed the hose from the main part of the hoover, so the poor Sister Sheila was hoovering for about 20 minutes without making a dent in cleaning the floor! She thought the hoover wasn't working properly before seeing the two friends falling around laughing at this. She ended up seeing the funny side of it... because luckily, it was not Thursday.

While Stephen had mostly a fun time in school, the bullying was a very tough part for him. The children who bully others usually prey on their victim's weakness and difference, which in Stephen's case was that he was small for his age and had to wear glasses. But these shouldn't be seen as weaknesses and shouldn't matter. Stephen also had a lot of good qualities that the bullies were not so obvious to bring up, likely because they were jealous of these qualities.

So remember this: bullying makes everybody feel bad, especially the victim and it can affect confidence for a long time after the bullying. You should always treat people the way you would like to be treated, and stand up to bullies if you see it, even if it is not you being bullied. Above all, be kind.

The End

Acknowledgements

Big thank you to all the people who supported me in writing this book. My children Luke, Kate & Ryan, they gave me the inspiration to write it, so thanks a million. Also my wife Lisa, who is always 100% behind me.

About the Author

Mark L'estrange is an author and podcast host from Dublin. *Adventures of Larry Lamppost & Friends*, his first book, is a collection of bedtime stories for children.

Written for his own children, the stories proved very popular in the L'estrange household. Mark was encouraged by friends and family to turn them into a book. The result is a fun collection of children's bedtime stories, packed with laughs, shocks and wacky characters.

Mark also runs a popular weekly podcast series called 'Authors Tuesday', which has a different author and subject every week. Previous guests have included Irish novelist Mary Bradford and best-selling Brazilian children's author Heloisa Prieto, to name but a few. Mark's Authors Tuesday podcast can be found on Spotify.

Printed in Great Britain
by Amazon

79126487R00058